W9-BRJ-708

THE
ZOOPHABET
NEEDLEWORK
BOOK

855 143 164 527 314 017 587 014 550 242 342 652 436 556 132 172 440 748 659 145 755 433 **A**	132 145 436 247 527 123 134 960 810 164 754 738 748 433 556 659 134 550 738 587 **B**	342 247 960 017 569 242 172 014 438 164 659 440 433 653 137 587 556 455 550 **C**	440 852 754 556 133 733 164 436 433 256 017 032 755 455 527 550 733 **D**
145 550 419 891 014 433 017 164 172 032 342 556 432 260 256 891 **E**	145 527 247 132 891 260 733 314 531 164 440 550 652 172 **F**	314 260 587 247 248 440 960 134 438 342 642 550 017 164 754 738 **G**	017 283 642 132 550 164 242 260 455 247 738 960 527 531 652 556 **H**
017 014 314 172 260 659 652 738 527 507 032 **I**	314 323 248 436 050 631 738 652 733 527 960 530 014 323 **J**	507 247 570 556 145 527 738 631 134 433 242 440 143 017 139 960 754 242 **K**	852 123 570 164 433 017 247 960 260 652 132 530 755 **L**
531 570 569 164 314 587 145 247 256 754 527 419 133 132 436 017 570 396 436 **M**	455 164 631 513 530 570 527 162 433 342 205 134 247 133 178 754 137 **N**	570 531 123 527 164 419 652 134 178 172 447 014 733 396 **O**	587 145 631 570 569 440 755 014 050 748 891 032 172 134 738 455 **P**
172 017 123 570 587 419 256 530 014 631 755 531 550 137 396 755 **Q**	032 178 242 440 172 891 164 050 507 134 240 810 530 164 050 **R**	172 134 050 032 248 164 032 133 419 507 440 810 455 017 570 260 **S**	531 143 631 733 242 314 455 017 810 123 527 247 396 960 **T**
419 164 323 283 433 440 032 631 137 570 440 274 513 248 132 396 891 **U**	587 754 530 570 455 178 642 440 323 132 164 247 455 556 342 **V**	531 123 143 134 172 419 530 527 436 440 247 396 145 032 570 017 178 164 256 133 137 642 **W**	570 653 436 527 531 455 133 755 178 017 631 550 137 283 **X**
	248 419 455 550 440 447 960 447 530 134 570 396 659 **Y**	530 419 032 569 178 260 570 631 960 032 527 587 455 550 631 **Z**	

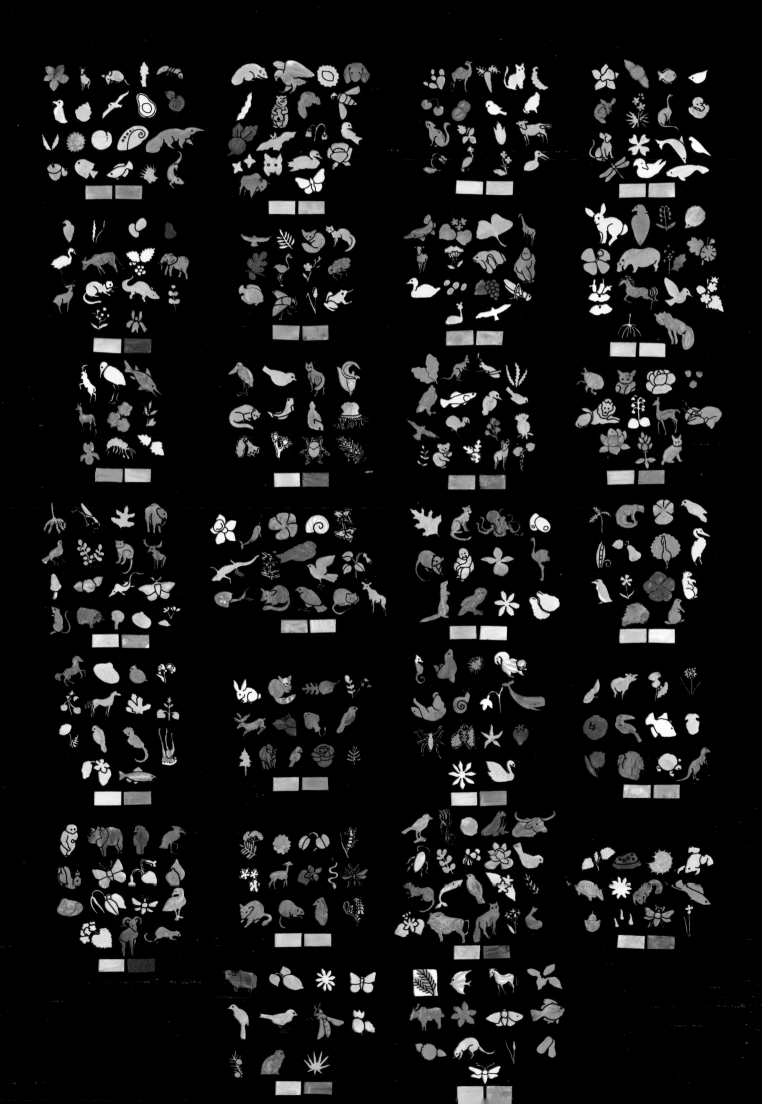

THE ZOOPHABET NEEDLEWORK BOOK

AN ALPHABET FOR NEEDLEWORKERS

Ăl′pha-bet, *n.* [Lat. *alphabetum*, Gr. ἀλφάβητος, from ἄλφα and βῆτα, the first two Greek letters; Fr. & Pr. *alphabet*.] The letters of a language arranged in the customary order; the series of letters which form the elements of written language.

Ăl′pha-bet, *v. t.* [*imp.* & *p. p.* ALPHABETED; *p. pr.* & *vb. n.* ALPHABETING.] To arrange in the order of an alphabet; to designate by the letters of the alphabet.

Ăl′pha-bet-ā′ri-an, *n.* A learner of the alphabet; an abecedarian. *Abp. Sancroft.*

Ăl′pha-bĕt′ic, } *a.* 1. Pertaining to, furnished
Ăl′pha-bĕt′ic al, } with, expressed by, or in the order of, the letters of the alphabet; as, *alphabetical* characters, *alphabetical* writing, an *alphabetical* language or arrangement.

COMPILED BY LESLIE TILLETT

Thomas Y. Crowell Company
Established 1834
New York

BOOKS BY THE AUTHOR

The Fall of the Aztecs

American Needlework 1776–1976

Wind on the Buffalo Grass

The Zoophabet Needlework Book:
AN ALPHABET FOR NEEDLEWORKERS

For E. C. F.

Acknowledgments
My assistant, Victoria Negrin, has been a great help, and the work of P. J.
Wynne made my concept a reality.

Copyright © 1977 by Leslie Tillett

All rights reserved.
Except for use in a review,
the reproduction or utilization of this work in
any form or by any electronic, mechanical, or
other means, now known or hereafter invented,
including xerography, photocopying,
and recording, and in any information storage
and retrieval system is forbidden without the
written permission of the publisher.
Published simultaneously in Canada
by Fitzhenry & Whiteside Limited, Toronto.

Designed by Lynn Braswell

Manufactured in the United States of America

Library of Congress Cataloging in Publication Data

Tillett, Leslie, 1915–
   The zoophabet needlework book.
      1. Needlework—Patterns. 2. Alphabets. 3. Animals.
I. Title.
TT753.T55   746.4'4   76-45763
ISBN 0-690-01211-X

1 2 3 4 5 6 7 8 9 10

PREFACE

The first alphabet was developed fully about the year 2000 B.C. Since then alphabets have been in a constant state of change. One of the earliest alphabets looked like this:

As with most basic design shapes, the technique used in inscribing the letters largely determined their form. In this case, a hand-held stylus that engraved soft clay gradually guided the developing shapes. Evolution applies to design as well as to animals, but in the long history of handwriting, technique has changed very slowly.

The Benedictines, that monastic order that protected so much of our Greco-Roman heritage during the Dark Ages, had the time to develop many beautiful scripts. They also helped develop the illuminated letter, to which I am so indebted in this effort.

After Gutenberg invented the movable-type press (although in fact the Chinese had had it centuries earlier), the designing of typefaces raced ahead over a widening horizon. The mechanics of old-style printing are such that almost any variation of design can be reproduced; the great number of typefaces that proliferated after 1452 proves that. However, the newest technical changes, such as incorporated in the linotype machine, can best handle only certain kinds of faces. The recent automation of the printing process is still more restrictive. The most recent technical innovation is the computer-printer, and no aesthetic considerations entered into the designing of its alphabet:

```
<Z1>super #L cies, skin   308-10255 MORE NUMBER
```

The typewriter has greatly eroded the ability to write by hand. Penmanship will soon be practiced only by specialists, similar to the paid village scribes once found in the Middle East. As the cost of casting a set of keys specially for one typewriter is decreasing, we shall all soon be able, it is hoped, to type our own personal script.

In penmanship, as in all handwork, "survival of the simplest" is the rule. A likely development of our roman alphabet is given here:

Λ3CƆⅭΓGⱵlJ⟨LⲘⲚOPQRSTUⅤⱲXZ

It must be said that the mechanical book-reading machine is now practical and will soon be in production for the blind. How long after that will it be before we shall all want one? Considering the overuse of the human eye for close work that our civilization demands, it may well be a good idea to have our reading done by a machine.

I chose animals as the main source for the designs in this book because they are our companions on this planet, and only a widespread awareness of this fact can stop them from being killed off. When our species advanced from gathering seeds and edible weeds to hunting, it did indeed make progress; but since then agriculture and now industry have enclosed or driven off, and gradually exterminated, many species of animals. This process goes on all over the world—and alongside of it the dilettante hunter still hunts.

Consult the Color Guide for a possible combination for your work, and bear in mind that the entire alphabet is embodied in this chart. Each figure in the Guide relates specifically to the larger illustration of the same figure within the book. The left-hand rectangle represents the color of the background inside the letter; the right-hand rectangle shows the color of the main background. The numbers given in the Guide refer to Paternayan Persian wool colors. But do not make final color decisions until you see the actual yarn at a shop. Remember that the Guide is printed in inks that can only approximate the colors of the yarns, and so is only meant to suggest what colors to use—season to taste, as it were.

The size of the letters can be enlarged or reduced. By far the easiest way is to have it done by a commercial photostater. Get prices before ordering the work—costs can vary between different firms.

Since this alphabet is intended for needleworkers of considerable experience and dexterity, it was designed with an ample supply of built-in options. Consider some of the following:

• Embroider the letters on cloth. Work in favorite stitches with threads of wool, cotton, linen, or silk. Or use only back, stem, or outline stitch for all of the embroidery. Choose a full range of colors or of tones of one color, or a single tone of a color.

• Embroider the letters on canvas using Continental, Basket Weave, or the straight stitches of Bargello techniques. Or use a combination of any or all. Overstitch detail on needlepoint using thread of another fiber for change of texture; back, stem, or outline stitch works well for this.

• If you choose the Crewel techniques, think of appliqué. Embroider on a smooth fabric, then sew or embroider the letter onto a textured backing. (There are many softbound books, available at variety and art needlework stores and departments, that cover this phase of work well and inexpensively.) Another way of accomplishing this combination is to transfer the design to nylon or cotton organdie or an even-weave scrim; baste the scrim to your background fabric, embroider through both thicknesses, then ravel the scrim.

• In somewhat the same manner, cross-stitch canvas can be used by needlepoint devotees. After the design is transferred to the canvas, baste the canvas to the background cloth, embroider through both thicknesses using canvas techniques, then ravel the canvas (see "Aids and Abettors").

• Do not feel that all of the detail within the outline of a letter must be used. Select whatever flora and fauna have greatest appeal and will best suit your abilities and the end use of your handwork. Eliminating some of the fine drawing leaves room for a textured stitch around the letter on canvas—perhaps Brick, Scotch, or Basket Weave.

FABRICS   Because of the fine detail within each letter, an 18-mesh canvas is suggested for the needlepoint. Naturally, the finer the canvas mesh, the more detail can be stitched in. Some effective pieces have been worked on 12-mesh canvas, however, by eliminating background drawing within the outline of the letter.

For embroidery, a smooth cloth of some stability seems best. Fine even-weave cottons or linens are good. Linen twill works well for fine embroidery; or consider wool challis or albatross with, if necessary, a thin lining fabric under it (work through both thicknesses), or even a silk with some body.

OTHER SUPPLIES   You will need good-quality tracing paper, a waterproof transfer pencil, waterproof pens and/or markers (very fine-line) or laundry marking pens, an iron, and rustproof pins and tacks or pushpins for blocking canvas. Art supply shops have most of these items. The Joan Moshimer Pattern Pencil is suggested since it will not bleed onto embroidery when wet. Test all supplies first on the fabrics with which they will be used. The starch in canvas can loosen some otherwise fast dyes. Test all fabrics for tolerance to iron heat. Be sure to read and follow the instructions that come with the transfer pencil, if it is used.

TRANSFERRING THE DESIGN   There are many methods for transferring designs to cloth or canvas; the two described here seem best suited to home use. Whichever method you decide to use, first trace the letter onto tracing paper with a black fine-line marker or pen. If the size is to be altered photostatically, it can be done from the tracing. For the first method, make a tracing of the stat as well.

Next, cut the canvas at least 3 inches larger, in both length and width, than the desired finished size of the project. Cut the cloth for embroidery 1 1/2 to 2 inches larger than the finished size. If the embroidered letter will be appliquéd to another background, the embroidery fabric can be about 1 1/2 inches longer and wider than the overall dimensions of the letter. In some way, protect the cut edges of canvas or cloth from raveling—binding with cloth or masking tape for canvas, stitching or cloth tape for embroidery fabric.

Method I Place the tracing face down on a light sheet of paper or tape it wrong side up to a windowpane. On the wrong side go over the lines of the tracing with a well-pointed transfer pencil. Be sure the lines are completely covered.

Pin or baste the tracing in position on the cloth or canvas so that it will not slip or shift. Following the instructions that come with the pencil, iron the letter onto the canvas or cloth.

(Don't use a steam iron—it will pucker the tracing.) Do not glide the iron over the tracing or you will get a blurred image; lift the iron and then lower it to the next position on the tracing.

When the design has been transferred, you may wish to darken some of the lines with a marker. If your color scheme is light, use a gray instead of a black marker on canvas so as not to darken the colors of the wools. On cloth, use a pen—a fine black line will not discolor the threads in the same way. If the work is exposed to light for any length of time, the transfer lines may fade and will need darkening.

Method II If you are working with a photostat, hold the fabric over it, right side up, against a window to see if the light comes through enough for tracing. If not, retrace the stat as before. Then tape the stat or tracing right side up on a bright, clean windowpane. Position the cloth or canvas over it and tape in place. Then trace the design with pen or marker on the canvas or cloth (pen might be better on cloth).

Blocking Unless a frame has been used for the needlepoint, canvas embroidery will need blocking. For this too there are many methods. One of them follows.

FINISHING THE WORK

Remove masking tape if it was used and brush a narrow band of waterproof glue around the cut edges. Tack a sheet of clear plastic to a wooden or Homosote board that is several inches larger around than the piece of canvas. Smooth a bath towel over the plastic and tack at the corners. Now tack the needlework face down to the board, pulling the embroidery into square position (a boxtop is good for checking right angles at the corners).

Set the tacks in the unworked canvas margin about 3/4 inch apart. Place a bath towel well dampened with warm water over the embroidery, and cover it with another sheet of plastic until the dampness permeates the needlework. Then remove the top plastic sheet, leaving the damp towel in place until it and the embroidery are thoroughly dry—about three or four days, depending on the weather. Some work may require several blockings to straighten it.

If the needlepoint is so warped it cannot be pulled square, roll it in a damp towel until it is quite wet, then tack it to the board as described above. Keep the work damp while pulling it straight, but use only a damp towel on top—a plastic sheet will not be needed.

If the work has a raised or textured surface, block it face up in the same manner as above.

Pressing For Crewel or embroidery on cloth that is only rumpled, pressing will usually finish the job. In the same manner as instructed above, prepare a well-padded board. Tack the embroidery face down to the board around the edges of the cloth.

What is done next depends on the base fabric of the embroidery. If it is silk, cover the back of the work with a smooth cloth and gently press, using a dry iron (silk may water-spot). Apply the iron slowly and lightly, over and over again, rather than using its full weight. Cotton, linen, or wool can be steamed. Use a damp cloth, or a steam iron and a thin dry cloth. Press lightly, never allowing the weight of the iron to rest on the embroidery or the base fabric.

AIDS AND ABETTORS

• Frames are helpful in preventing canvas embroidery from warping, by keeping an even tension. Crewel embroidery will not pucker or rumple during the course of the work if framed. Use artist's canvas stretchers or frames with a rotating dowel at top and bottom. For embroidery on cloth that is not of a counted-thread type, hoops can be used. All frames call for a two-handed technique—one hand over the work, the other under the work to return the needle to the top. One hand can do both jobs, but the project takes longer that way.

• Delicate fabrics and already embroidered areas should be protected from hoops with tissue both over and under the fabric. Embroidery of all types should be protected in the same way when rolled up on a rotating dowel; use thin sheets of plastic or tissue.

• If you use cross-stitch canvas, first transfer the design to it as described above. Then iron the canvas between sheets of kitchen wax paper several times. Remove the excess wax by pressing the canvas between sheets of tissue. Be sure to test that the waxed canvas will not stain your basic fabric. The waxing helps prevent roughing of embroidery threads when the canvas is raveled.

Baste the canvas to the cloth, aligning it with warp and filling threads of the cloth. Use many rows of basting to keep the canvas from shifting. Any of the canvas embroidery stitches can be employed.

To ravel the canvas, trim it to within about 2 inches of the embroidery all around. Pull out one canvas thread at a time up to the stitching. Ease out the canvas threads under the narrowest parts of the stitching first; tweezers or fine crochet hooks are helpful for this. And, yes, indeed, raveling the canvas takes more patience than working the embroidery.

• If you are stitching over organdie as a temporary canvas, be assured that raveling it is a much more simple task, though still exacting. Baste thoroughly in the same manner as directed above. With nylon organdie particularly, there is no need to wax.

• If you are working on a silk fabric, use silk for basting and fine sewing needles for pinning; these will not mar the cloth as much as pins and cotton basting.

● In canvas embroidery, a smoother result is accomplished by bringing the needle to the face of the work through an empty space in the canvas, then down to the wrong side through a space that has one stitch. The stitch already worked is evened in this process, instead of being slightly uprooted as would occur if the needle came up to the face in its space.

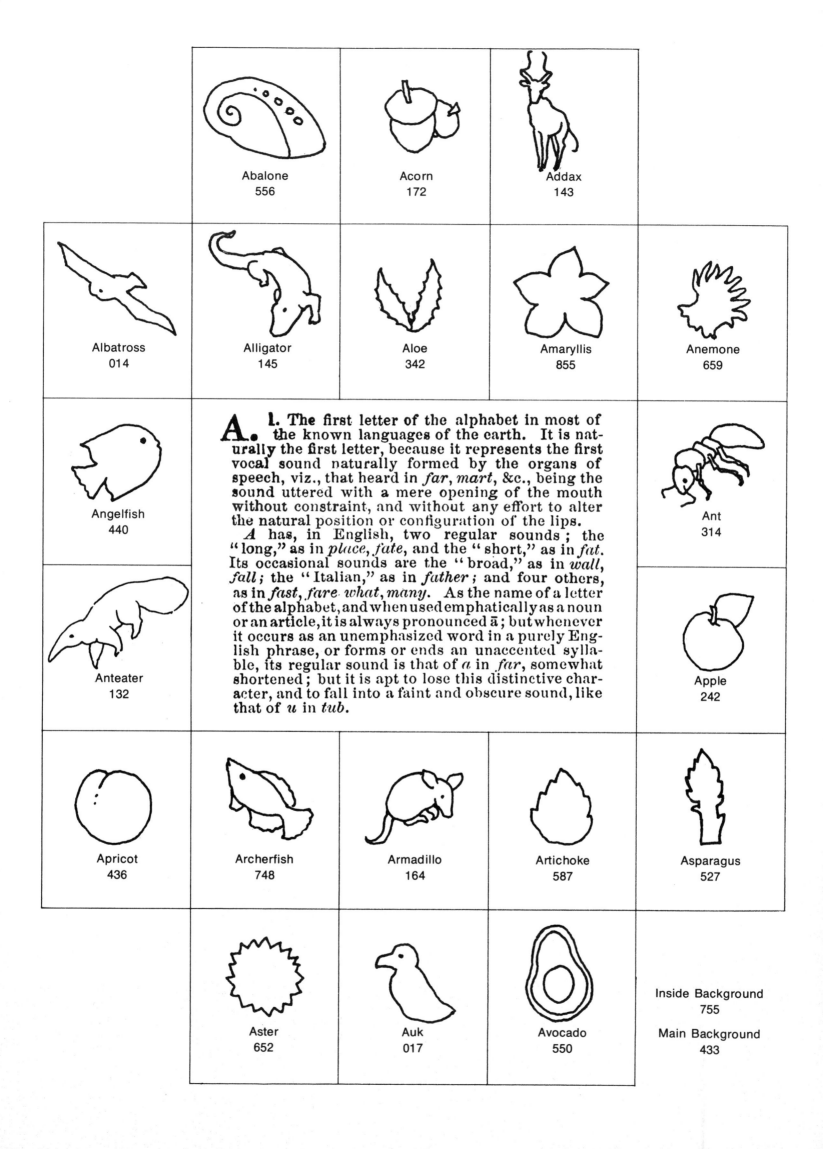

Abalone
556

Acorn
172

Addax
143

Albatross
014

Alligator
145

Aloe
342

Amaryllis
855

Anemone
659

Angelfish
440

Ant
314

Anteater
132

A. 1. The first letter of the alphabet in most of the known languages of the earth. It is naturally the first letter, because it represents the first vocal sound naturally formed by the organs of speech, viz., that heard in *far, mart,* &c., being the sound uttered with a mere opening of the mouth without constraint, and without any effort to alter the natural position or configuration of the lips.

A has, in English, two regular sounds; the "long," as in *place, fate,* and the "short," as in *fat.* Its occasional sounds are the "broad," as in *wall, fall;* the "Italian," as in *father;* and four others, as in *fast, fare what, many.* As the name of a letter of the alphabet, and when used emphatically as a noun or an article, it is always pronounced ā; but whenever it occurs as an unemphasized word in a purely English phrase, or forms or ends an unaccented syllable, its regular sound is that of *a* in *far,* somewhat shortened; but it is apt to lose this distinctive character, and to fall into a faint and obscure sound, like that of *u* in *tub.*

Apple
242

Apricot
436

Archerfish
748

Armadillo
164

Artichoke
587

Asparagus
527

Aster
652

Auk
017

Avocado
550

Inside Background
755

Main Background
433

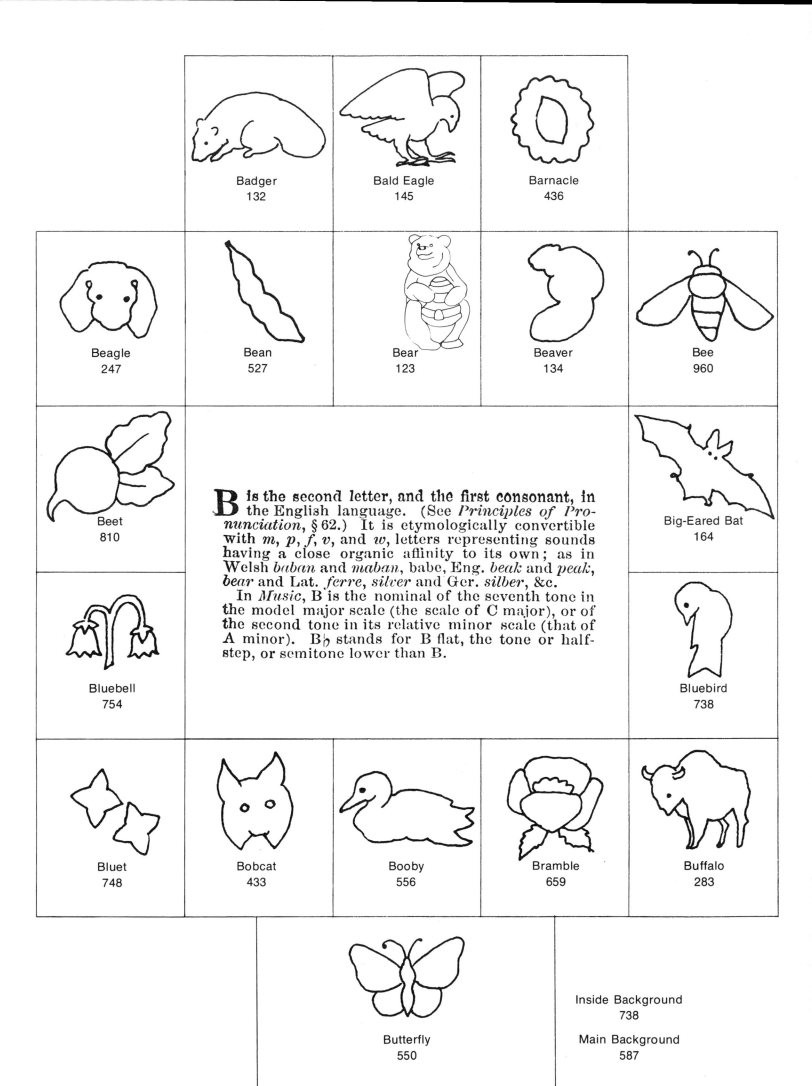

Badger
132

Bald Eagle
145

Barnacle
436

Beagle
247

Bean
527

Bear
123

Beaver
134

Bee
960

Beet
810

B is the second letter, and the first consonant, in the English language. (See *Principles of Pronunciation*, § 62.) It is etymologically convertible with *m*, *p*, *f*, *v*, and *w*, letters representing sounds having a close organic affinity to its own; as in Welsh *baban* and *maban*, babe, Eng. *beak* and *peak*, *bear* and Lat. *ferre*, *silver* and Ger. *silber*, &c.

In *Music*, B is the nominal of the seventh tone in the model major scale (the scale of C major), or of the second tone in its relative minor scale (that of A minor). B♭ stands for B flat, the tone or half-step, or semitone lower than B.

Big-Eared Bat
164

Bluebell
754

Bluebird
738

Bluet
748

Bobcat
433

Booby
556

Bramble
659

Buffalo
283

Butterfly
550

Inside Background
738

Main Background
587

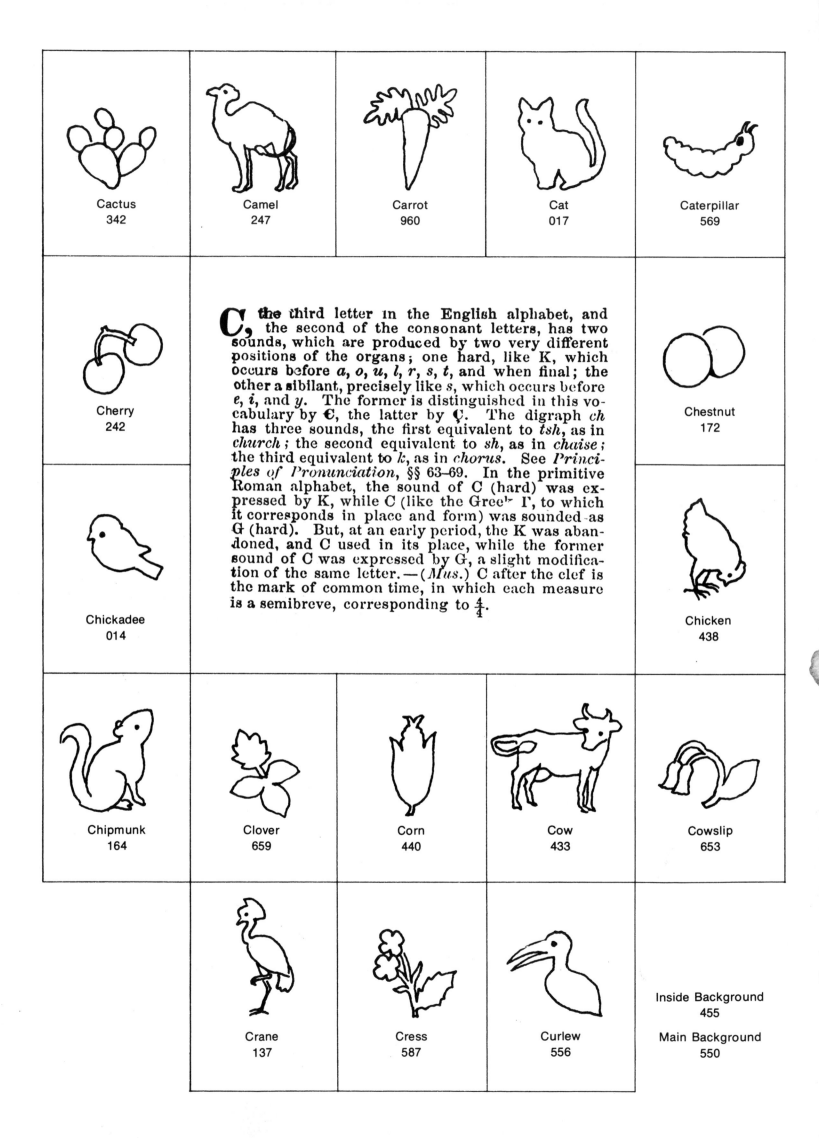

Cactus
342

Camel
247

Carrot
960

Cat
017

Caterpillar
569

Cherry
242

Chestnut
172

C, the third letter in the English alphabet, and the second of the consonant letters, has two sounds, which are produced by two very different positions of the organs; one hard, like K, which occurs before *a, o, u, l, r, s, t,* and when final; the other a sibilant, precisely like *s,* which occurs before *e, i,* and *y.* The former is distinguished in this vocabulary by Ꞓ, the latter by Ç. The digraph *ch* has three sounds, the first equivalent to *tsh,* as in *church*; the second equivalent to *sh,* as in *chaise*; the third equivalent to *k,* as in *chorus.* See *Principles of Pronunciation,* §§ 63–69. In the primitive Roman alphabet, the sound of C (hard) was expressed by K, while C (like the Greek Γ, to which it corresponds in place and form) was sounded as G (hard). But, at an early period, the K was abandoned, and C used in its place, while the former sound of C was expressed by G, a slight modification of the same letter.—(*Mus.*) C after the clef is the mark of common time, in which each measure is a semibreve, corresponding to $\frac{4}{4}$.

Chickadee
014

Chicken
438

Chipmunk
164

Clover
659

Corn
440

Cow
433

Cowslip
653

Crane
137

Cress
587

Curlew
556

Inside Background
455

Main Background
550

Daffodil
440

Dahlia
852

Damselfish
754

Daphnia
556

Deer
133

D, in the English alphabet, is the fourth letter, and the third consonant or articulation.

Delphinium
733

Dinosaur
164

Dodo
436

Dog
433

Dogwood
256

Dolphin
017

Dove
032

Dragonfly
755

Duck
455

Dugong
527

Inside Background
550

Main Background
733

Eagle
145

Eelgrass
550

Egg
419

Eggplant
891

Egret
014

E. The second vowel and the fifth letter of the English alphabet. It occurs more frequently in the words of the language than any other letter of the alphabet. It has two principal sounds, the long, as in *me*, and the short, as in *met*: also, several occasional sounds, the three principal of which are heard in the words *heir, prey, err*, respectively. At the end of words it is usually silent, but serves to indicate that the preceding vowel has its long sound, where otherwise it would be short, as in *māne, cāne, mēte*, which without the final *e* would be pronounced *măn, căn, mět*. After *c* and *g*, the final *e* indicates that these letters are to be pronounced as *s* and *j*, respectively, as in *laçe, raĝe*, which, without *e*, would be pronounced *lac, rag*. See *Principles of Pronunciation*, §§ 10–14, 46, and 47. — (*Mus.*) E is the third tone of the model diatonic scale. E♭ (E flat) is a tone intermediate between D and E.

Eland
433

Elderberry
017

Elephant
164

Elk
172

Ermine
032

Eryops
342

Eucalyptus
556

Everlasting
432

Eyebright
260

Inside Background
256

Main Background
891

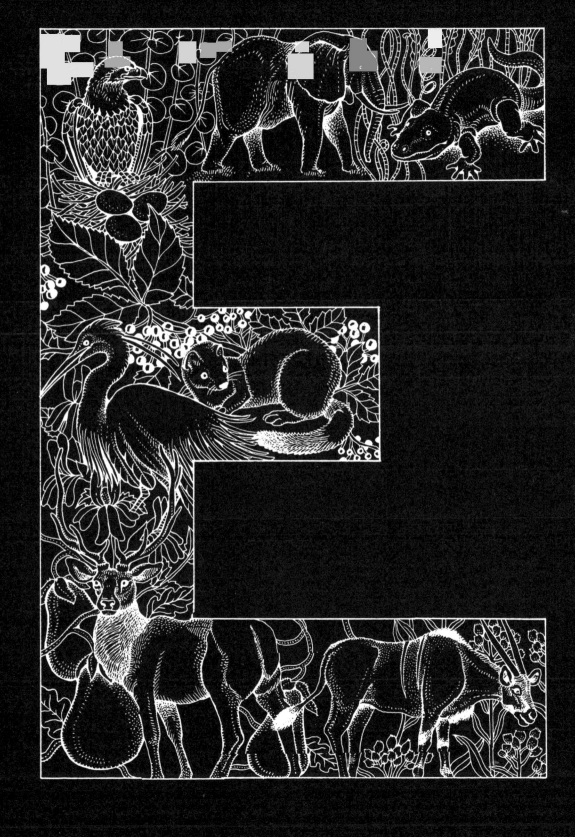

Falcon
145

Fern
527

Ferrec Fox
247

Ferret
132

Fig
891

F, the sixth letter of the English alphabet, is a labio dental articulation, formed by the passage of breath between the lower lip and the upper incisive teeth or between the upper lip and the lower incisive teeth. By most persons it is produced in the former manner. See *Principles of Pronunciation,* § 71. Its corresponding sonant letter is *v,* in producing which voice is substituted for breath The figure of the letter F is the same as that of the Eolic digamma [F], to which it is also closely related in power. See DIGAMMA. In etymologies, F is convertible with various other letters, especially the labials. In music, F is the fourth tone of the gamut, or model scale. F sharp (F♯) is a tone intermediate between F and G. In chronology, F is one of the seven dominical letters. In heraldry, it denotes the nombril or navel point in an escutcheon.

Flamingo
260

Flax
733

Flea
314

Flounder
531

Fly
164

Foxtail
440

Frog
550

Inside Background
652

Main Background
172

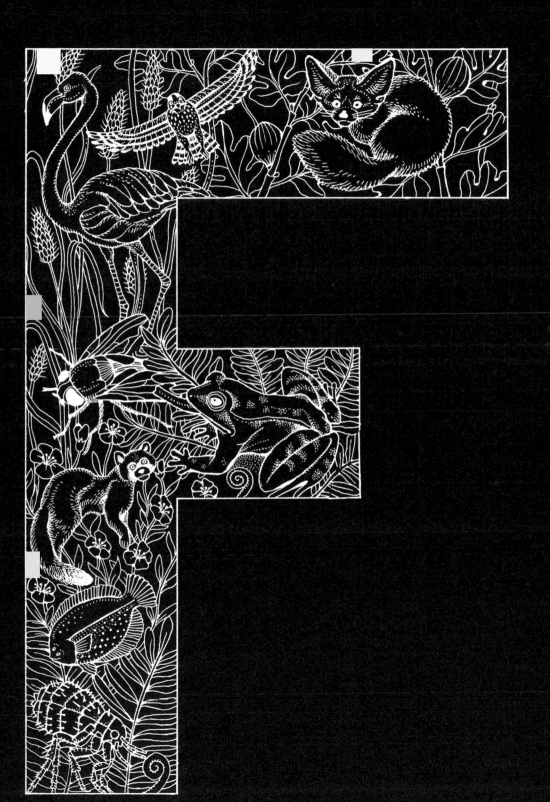

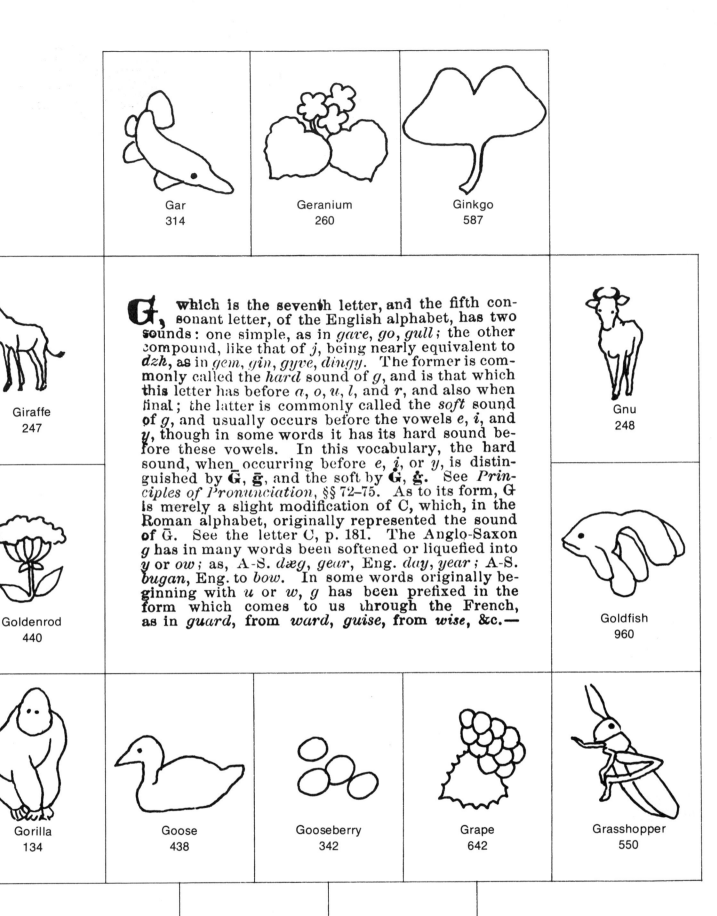

Gar
314

Geranium
260

Ginkgo
587

Giraffe
247

G, which is the seventh letter, and the fifth consonant letter, of the English alphabet, has two sounds: one simple, as in *gave, go, gull*; the other compound, like that of *j*, being nearly equivalent to *dzh*, as in *gem, gin, gyve, dingy*. The former is commonly called the *hard* sound of *g*, and is that which this letter has before *a, o, u, l*, and *r*, and also when final; the latter is commonly called the *soft* sound of *g*, and usually occurs before the vowels *e, i*, and *y*, though in some words it has its hard sound before these vowels. In this vocabulary, the hard sound, when occurring before *e, i*, or *y*, is distinguished by Ḡ, ḡ, and the soft by G̣, g̣. See *Principles of Pronunciation*, §§ 72–75. As to its form, G is merely a slight modification of C, which, in the Roman alphabet, originally represented the sound of Ḡ. See the letter C, p. 181. The Anglo-Saxon *g* has in many words been softened or liquefied into *y* or *ow*; as, A-S. *dæg, gear*, Eng. *day, year*; A-S. *bugan*, Eng. to *bow*. In some words originally beginning with *u* or *w, g* has been prefixed in the form which comes to us through the French, as in *guard*, from *ward*, *guise*, from *wise*, &c.—

Gnu
248

Goldenrod
440

Goldfish
960

Gorilla
134

Goose
438

Gooseberry
342

Grape
642

Grasshopper
550

Grebe
017

Gull
164

Inside Background
754

Main Background
738

Hare
017

Hawk
283

Heather
642

Hedgehog
132

Henbane
550

Hibiscus
960

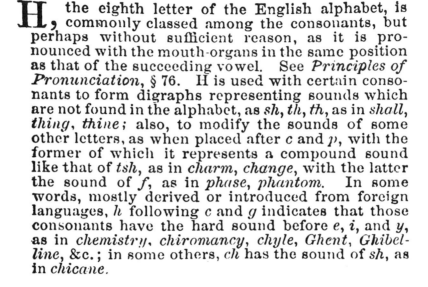

H, the eighth letter of the English alphabet, is commonly classed among the consonants, but perhaps without sufficient reason, as it is pronounced with the mouth-organs in the same position as that of the succeeding vowel. See *Principles of Pronunciation,* § 76. H is used with certain consonants to form digraphs representing sounds which are not found in the alphabet, as *sh, th, th,* as in *shall, thing, thine;* also, to modify the sounds of some other letters, as when placed after *c* and *p,* with the former of which it represents a compound sound like that of *tsh,* as in *charm, change,* with the latter the sound of *f,* as in *phase, phantom.* In some words, mostly derived or introduced from foreign languages, *h* following *c* and *g* indicates that those consonants have the hard sound before *e, i,* and *y,* as in *chemistry, chiromancy, chyle, Ghent, Ghibelline,* &c.; in some others, *ch* has the sound of *sh,* as in *chicane.*

Hippopotamus
164

Holly
242

Hollyhock
260

Honeysuckle
455

Horse
247

Hummingbird
738

Hydra
527

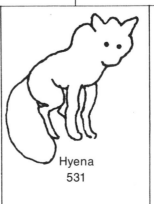

Hyena
531

Inside Background
652

Main Background
556

Ibex
017

Ibis
014

Ichthyosaur
314

Impala
172

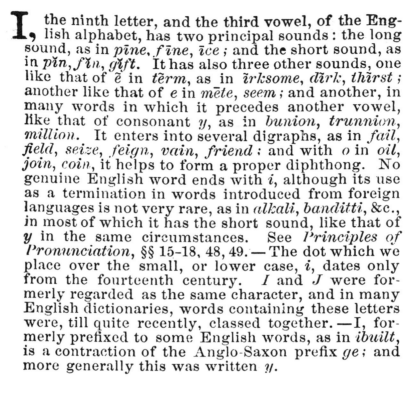

I, the ninth letter, and the third vowel, of the English alphabet, has two principal sounds: the long sound, as in *pīne, fīne, īce;* and the short sound, as in *pĭn, fĭn, gĭft.* It has also three other sounds, one like that of *ē* in *tērm,* as in *ĭrksome, dĭrk, thĭrst;* another like that of *e* in *mēte, seem;* and another, in many words in which it precedes another vowel, like that of consonant *y,* as in *bunion, trunnion, million.* It enters into several digraphs, as in *fail, field, seize, feign, vain, friend:* and with *o* in *oil, join, coin,* it helps to form a proper diphthong. No genuine English word ends with *i,* although its use as a termination in words introduced from foreign languages is not very rare, as in *alkali, banditti,* &c., in most of which it has the short sound, like that of *y* in the same circumstances. See *Principles of Pronunciation,* §§ 15-18, 48, 49. — The dot which we place over the small, or lower case, *i,* dates only from the fourteenth century. *I* and *J* were formerly regarded as the same character, and in many English dictionaries, words containing these letters were, till quite recently, classed together. — I, formerly prefixed to some English words, as in *ibuilt,* is a contraction of the Anglo-Saxon prefix *ge;* and more generally this was written *y.*

Impatiens
260

Iris
652

Iresine
659

Isopod
738

Ivy
527

Inside Background
507

Main Background
032

Jabiru
314

Jackal
248

Jackdaw
323

Jack-in-the-Pulpit
436

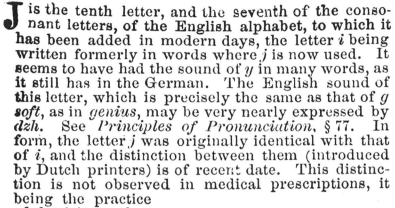

J is the tenth letter, and the seventh of the consonant letters, of the English alphabet, to which it has been added in modern days, the letter *i* being written formerly in words where *j* is now used. It seems to have had the sound of *y* in many words, as it still has in the German. The English sound of this letter, which is precisely the same as that of *g* soft, as in *genius*, may be very nearly expressed by *dzh*. See *Principles of Pronunciation*, § 77. In form, the letter *j* was originally identical with that of *i*, and the distinction between them (introduced by Dutch printers) is of recent date. This distinction is not observed in medical prescriptions, it being the practice of physicians, when the symbol for unity ends a series of numerals, to write *j* instead of *i*; as, *vj. vij, viij*, &c.

Jaguar
050

Jay
738

Jawfish
631

Jellyfish
652

Jimsonweed
733

Joshua Tree
527

Junebug
960

Juniper
530

Inside Background
014

Main Background
323

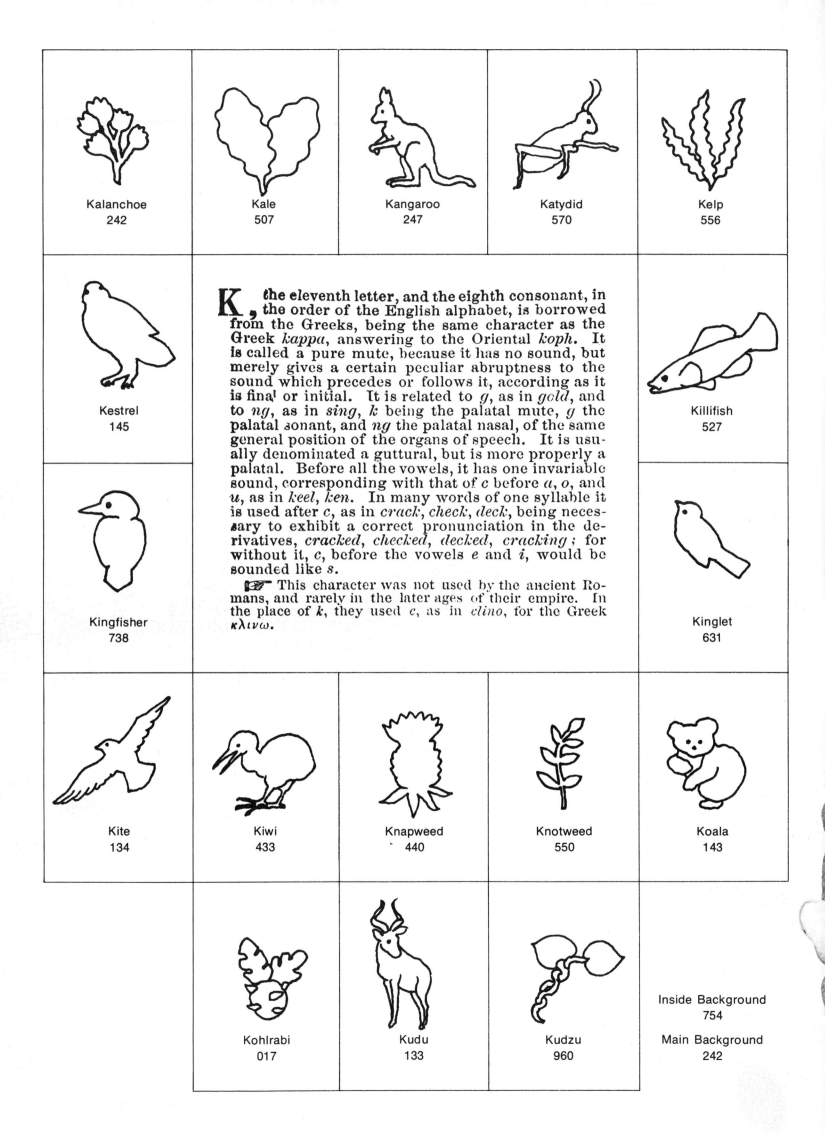

Kalanchoe
242

Kale
507

Kangaroo
247

Katydid
570

Kelp
556

Kestrel
145

Killifish
527

Kingfisher
738

K, the eleventh letter, and the eighth consonant, in the order of the English alphabet, is borrowed from the Greeks, being the same character as the Greek *kappa*, answering to the Oriental *koph*. It is called a pure mute, because it has no sound, but merely gives a certain peculiar abruptness to the sound which precedes or follows it, according as it is final or initial. It is related to *g*, as in *gold*, and to *ng*, as in *sing*, *k* being the palatal mute, *g* the palatal sonant, and *ng* the palatal nasal, of the same general position of the organs of speech. It is usually denominated a guttural, but is more properly a palatal. Before all the vowels, it has one invariable sound, corresponding with that of *c* before *a*, *o*, and *u*, as in *keel*, *ken*. In many words of one syllable it is used after *c*, as in *crack*, *check*, *deck*, being necessary to exhibit a correct pronunciation in the derivatives, *cracked*, *checked*, *decked*, *cracking*; for without it, *c*, before the vowels *e* and *i*, would be sounded like *s*.

☞ This character was not used by the ancient Romans, and rarely in the later ages of their empire. In the place of *k*, they used *c*, as in *clino*, for the Greek κλινω.

Kinglet
631

Kite
134

Kiwi
433

Knapweed
440

Knotweed
550

Koala
143

Kohlrabi
017

Kudu
133

Kudzu
960

Inside Background
754

Main Background
242

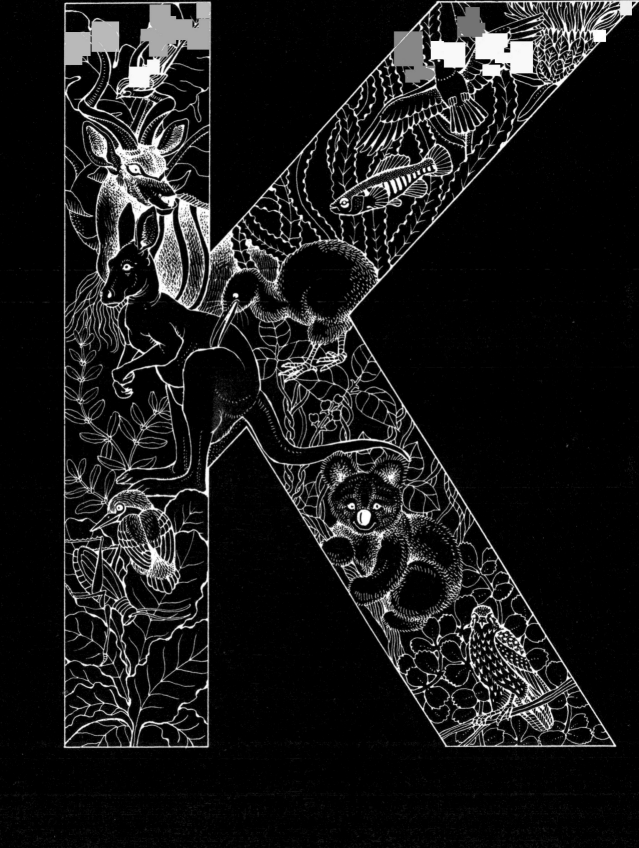

Ladybug
852

Lemur
123

Lettuce
570

Lichen
164

Lion
433

Lily-of-the-Valley
017

Llama
247

L, the twelfth letter of the English alphabet, is usually denominated a *semi-vowel*, or a *liquid*. Its shape is evidently borrowed from that of the Oriental *lamed*, or *lomad*, nearly coinciding with the Samaritan 𝌆. *L* has only one sound in English, as in *like, canal.* At the end of monosyllables, it is often doubled, as in *fall, full, tell, bell;* but not after diphthongs and digraphs, as in *foul, fool, prowl, growl, foal.* In English words, the terminating syllable *le* is unaccented, the *e* is silent, and *l* forms a syllable by itself, as in *able, eagle,* pronounced *abl, eegl.* [See *Prin. of Pron.*, § 79.] In etymologies, *l* is interchangeable with *r, n, m, d.*

Lobster
960

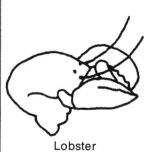

Lotus
260

Lupine
652

Lynx
132

Inside Background
530

Main Background
755

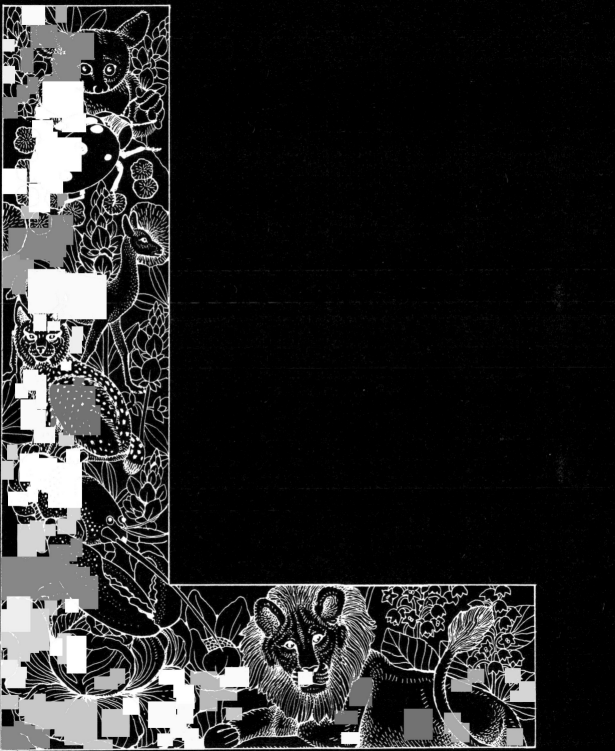

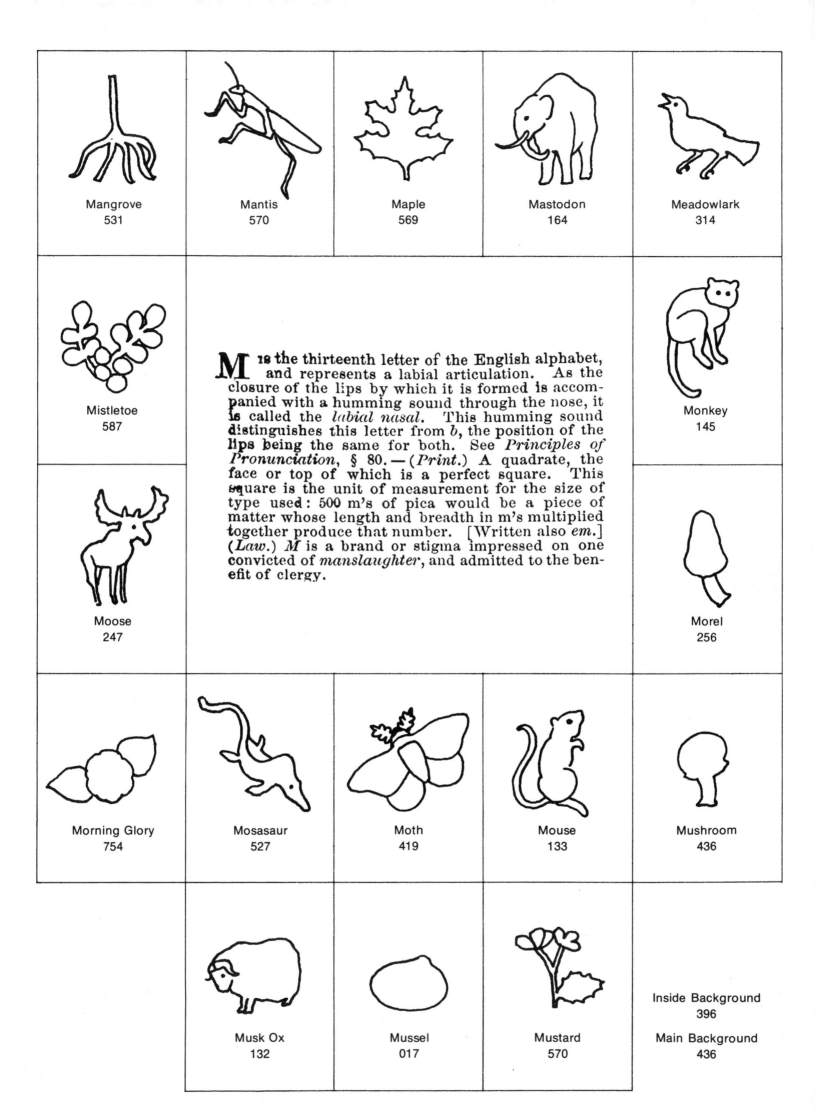

Mangrove
531

Mantis
570

Maple
569

Mastodon
164

Meadowlark
314

Mistletoe
587

Monkey
145

Moose
247

M is the thirteenth letter of the English alphabet, and represents a labial articulation. As the closure of the lips by which it is formed is accompanied with a humming sound through the nose, it is called the *labial nasal*. This humming sound distinguishes this letter from *b*, the position of the lips being the same for both. See *Principles of Pronunciation*, § 80. — (*Print.*) A quadrate, the face or top of which is a perfect square. This square is the unit of measurement for the size of type used: 500 m's of pica would be a piece of matter whose length and breadth in m's multiplied together produce that number. [Written also *em.*] (*Law.*) *M* is a brand or stigma impressed on one convicted of *manslaughter*, and admitted to the benefit of clergy.

Morel
256

Morning Glory
754

Mosasaur
527

Moth
419

Mouse
133

Mushroom
436

Musk Ox
132

Mussel
017

Mustard
570

Inside Background
396

Main Background
436

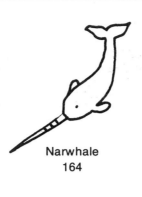

Narcissus
455

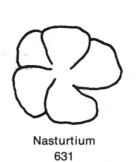

Narwhale
164

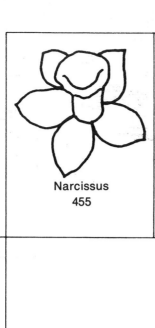

Nasturtium
631

Nautilus
513

Nettle
530

N, the fourteenth letter of the English alphabet, is a nasal consonant, and is formed by placing the end of the tongue against the root of the upper teeth, with the expulsion of a current of intonated or vocalized breath. Its principal sound is that heard in *b in, done, noon,* &c.; but when standing before *g* or *k,* or their equivalents, it has another sound, nearly represented by *ng,* as in *finger, brink,* &c. This is sometimes represented by *ng,* as in *singer.* When final after *m,* it is silent, as in *hymn* and *condemn.*

Newt
570

Niad
527

Nighthawk
162

Nightjar
433

Nightshade
342

Nilgai
178

Numbat
134

Nuthatch
247

Nutria
133

Inside Background
754

Main Background
137

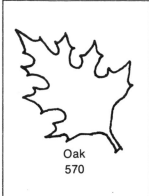

Oak
570

Ocelot
531

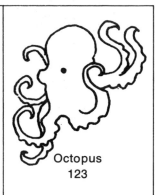

Octopus
123

Olive
527

Opossum
164

O, the fifteenth letter, and the fourth vowel, in the English alphabet, has several different sounds, the principal of which are, the long sound, heard in *tone*, *groan*, *old*; the short sound, heard in *lot*, *lodge*, *rod*; a sound like short *u*, as in *done*, *son*, *flood*; a sound like the German or Italian long *u*, or the French *ou*, as in *move*, *do*, *booty*; a similar but shorter sound, as in *wolf*, *book*, *foot*; and a sound like broad *a*, as in *form*, *mortal*. See *Principles of Pronunciation*, §§ 19–25, 50, 51. In Irish family names, *O* is equivalent to *son of*, and denotes progeny, or is a character of dignity; as, *O'Neil*; *O'Carrol*. Among the ancients, *O* was a mark of triple time, from the notion that the ternary, or number 3, is the most perfect of numbers, and properly expressed by a circle, the most perfect figure.

Orangutan
419

Orchid
652

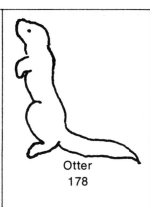

Ostrich
134

Otter
178

Owl
172

Oxeye Daisy
447

Oyster
014

Inside Background
733

Main Background
396

Palm
587

Pansy
631

Panther
145

Parakeet
570

P, the twelfth consonant, and the sixteenth letter in the order of the English alphabet, is formed by closely compressing the lips, and separating them suddenly with an explosive emission of breath, as in *part*, *pop*. P is called a pure mute, because it has no sound. Like the other pure mutes, *k* and *t*, it gives an abruptness to the sound which immediately precedes or follows it, according as it is itself final or initial in the syllable, as in *imp*, *play*. P is closely related to *b* and *m*, all three of these letters representing labial sounds, *p* being the labial mute, *b* the labial sonant, and *m* the labial nasal. P is convertible into *b* and *f*, and sometimes into *v*. The combination *ph* has the same sound as *f*, as in *philosophy*, being equivalent to the Gr. φ.

Pea
569

Peacock
755

Pear
440

Pelican
014

Penguin
050

Periwinkle
748

Petunia
891

Polar Bear
032

Porcupine
172

Prairie Dog
134

Inside Background
738

Main Background
455

Quagga
172

Quahog
017

Quail
123

Quaking Grass
570

Quandong
587

Q, the seventeenth letter of the English alphabet, has but one sound, which is the same as that of *k*, or *c hard*. It is, therefore, a superfluous letter. In English, it never ends a word, as it does in French and some other modern languages. It is always followed by *u*, the two letters together being pronounced like *kw*, except in some words in which the *u* is silent; as, *quake*, *quack*, *pique*, pronounced *kwake*, *kwack*, *peek*. In the Anglo-Saxon, this letter is not used, *cu*, or, more generally, *cw*, being employed instead of it; as in *cwic*, quick; *cwen*, queen. For *qu* in English, the Dutch use *kw*, the Germans *qu*, the Swedes and the Danes *qv*, which answer to our *kw*. The Gothic has a character which answers to *qu*. The English name of the letter, *cue*, is said to be from the French *queue*, a tail, the form being the same as that of O, with a tail added. Some, however, regard the form as a contraction of *cv* or *cu*.

Quarter Horse
419

Quartz
256

Quassia
530

Queen Anne's Lace
014

Quelea
631

Quetzal
755

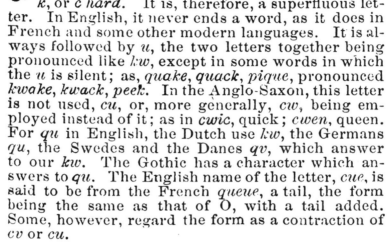

Quillwort
531

Quince
550

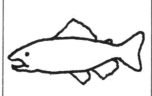

Quinnat
137

Inside Background
396

Main Background
755

Rabbit
032

Raccoon
178

Radish
242

Ragwort
440

Ray
164

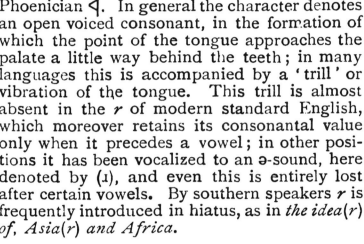

R (āɹ), the eighteenth letter of the modern and seventeenth of the ancient Roman alphabet, is derived through early Greek Ρ, Ρ from the Phoenician ᐸ. In general the character denotes an open voiced consonant, in the formation of which the point of the tongue approaches the palate a little way behind the teeth; in many languages this is accompanied by a 'trill' or vibration of the tongue. This trill is almost absent in the *r* of modern standard English, which moreover retains its consonantal value only when it precedes a vowel; in other positions it has been vocalized to an ə-sound, here denoted by (ɹ), and even this is entirely lost after certain vowels. By southern speakers *r* is frequently introduced in hiatus, as in *the idea(r) of, Asia(r) and Africa.*

Raspberry
891

Redwing Blackbird
050

Redwood
507

Reed
530

Reindeer
172

Rhinoceros
134

Robin
248

Rose
810

Inside Background
164

Main Background
050

Seahorse
172

Sea Lion
134

Sea Urchin
050

Skunk
032

Sloth
248

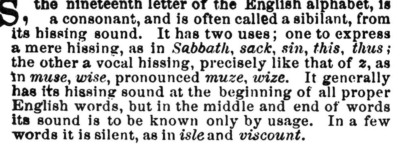

S, the nineteenth letter of the English alphabet, is a consonant, and is often called a sibilant, from its hissing sound. It has two uses; one to express a mere hissing, as in *Sabbath, sack, sin, this, thus;* the other a vocal hissing, precisely like that of **z,** as in *muse, wise,* pronounced *muze, wize.* It generally has its hissing sound at the beginning of all proper English words, but in the middle and end of words its sound is to be known only by usage. In a few words it is silent, as in *isle* and *viscount.*

Snail
164

Snowdrop
032

Sperm Whale
133

Spider
419

Spruce
507

Starfish
440

Strawberry
810

Sunflower
455

Swan
017

Inside Background
570

Main Background
260

Tadpole
531

Tapir
143

Thistle
631

Thrift
733

T, the twentieth letter of the English alphabet, is a simple consonant, allied to both *D* and *N*, all three of these letters being dental elements. It differs from *D* in the entire absence of vocality, and from *N* in the absence of a nasal as well as of a vocal quality. It is one of the three pure mutes (*k* and *p* being the other two), and is so called because it has no sound of its own, but merely serves to give an abruptness to the sound which immediately precedes or follows it in the same syllable. When *t* is followed by *h*, as in *think* and *that*, the combination really forms a distinct sound, for which we have no single character. This combination has two sounds in English; surd or whispered, as in *think*, and sonant or vocal, as in *that*. The letters *ti*, before a vowel, and unaccented, usually pass into the sound of *sh*, as in *nation, motion, partial*, which are pronounced *nashun, moshun, parshal*. In this case, *t* loses entirely its proper sound or use, and being blended with the subsequent letter, a new sound results from the combination, which is in fact a simple sound. If, however, *s* or *x* precedes, the combination *ti* has the sound of the English *ch*, as in *Christian, mixtion, question*. See *Principles of Pronunciation*, §§ 96—100. In etymology, *t* is interchangeable with *d*, and sometimes with *l, p, s,* and *th*.

Tomato
242

Toucan
314

Triggerfish
455

Trilobite
017

Tulip
810

Turkey
123

Turtle
527

Tyrannosaur
247

Inside Background
396

Main Background
960

Uakari
419

Uintatherium
164

Umbrella Bird
323

Umbrette
283

Unau
433

U is the twenty-first letter and the fifth vowel in the English alphabet. Its true primary sound, in Anglo-Saxon, was the sound which it still retains in most of the languages of Europe — that of *oo* in *cool, tool,* answering to the French *ou* in *tour.* This sound was changed to that heard in the words *use, tube,* &c., probably under the Norman kings, by the attempt made to introduce the Norman-French language into common use. Besides these two sounds, *u* has also two other sounds, as exemplified in the words *but, bull.* See *Principles of Pronunciation,* §§ 29–34, and §§ 52, 53. The letter *U* is a modification of the Greek letter ϒ. It has a close affinity to the consonant *v,* and hence these two letters were formerly confounded in writing and printing, the discrimination between them being of a comparatively recent date.

Underwing
440

Unicorn Plant
032

Unicorn Shell
631

Unios
137

Unona
570

Upholsterer Bee
440

Upland Goose
274

Uraursi
513

Urial
248

Urva
132

Inside Background
396

Main Background
891

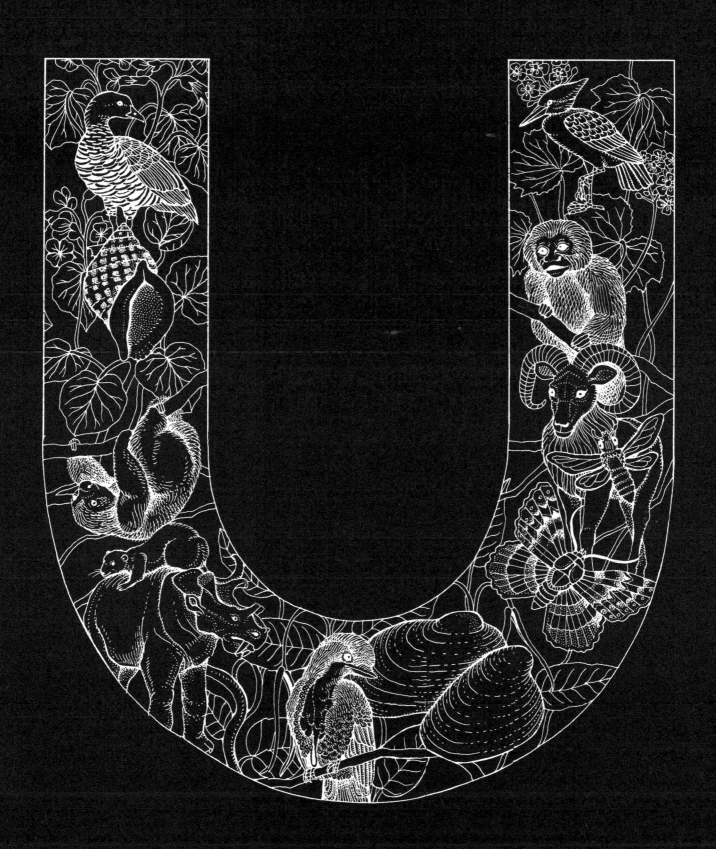

Valerian
587

Venidium
754

Venus's-Flytrap
530

Verbena
455

V, the twenty-second letter of the English alphabet, represents a uniform consonant sound, as heard in *vain, eve, vow,* and *move.* It is the vocal or sonant correspondent of *f.* Its form is only a variety of the character by which the vowel *U* is denoted, the latter being in its origin the cursive character employed with soft materials, while *V* is better adapted for writing on stone. The two letters were formerly used indiscriminately, the one for the other, and in some dictionaries and other works of reference they are still interchanged and confounded, though they have now as distinct uses as any other two letters in the alphabet. In etymology, *v* is interchangeable with *f, b,* and *m,* and also with *w, gu,* and *du.*

Vernal Grass
570

Vetch
455

Vicuna
178

Violet
642

Viper
440

Vipionid
323

Vizcacha
132

Vole
164

Vulture
247

Inside Background
556

Main Background
342

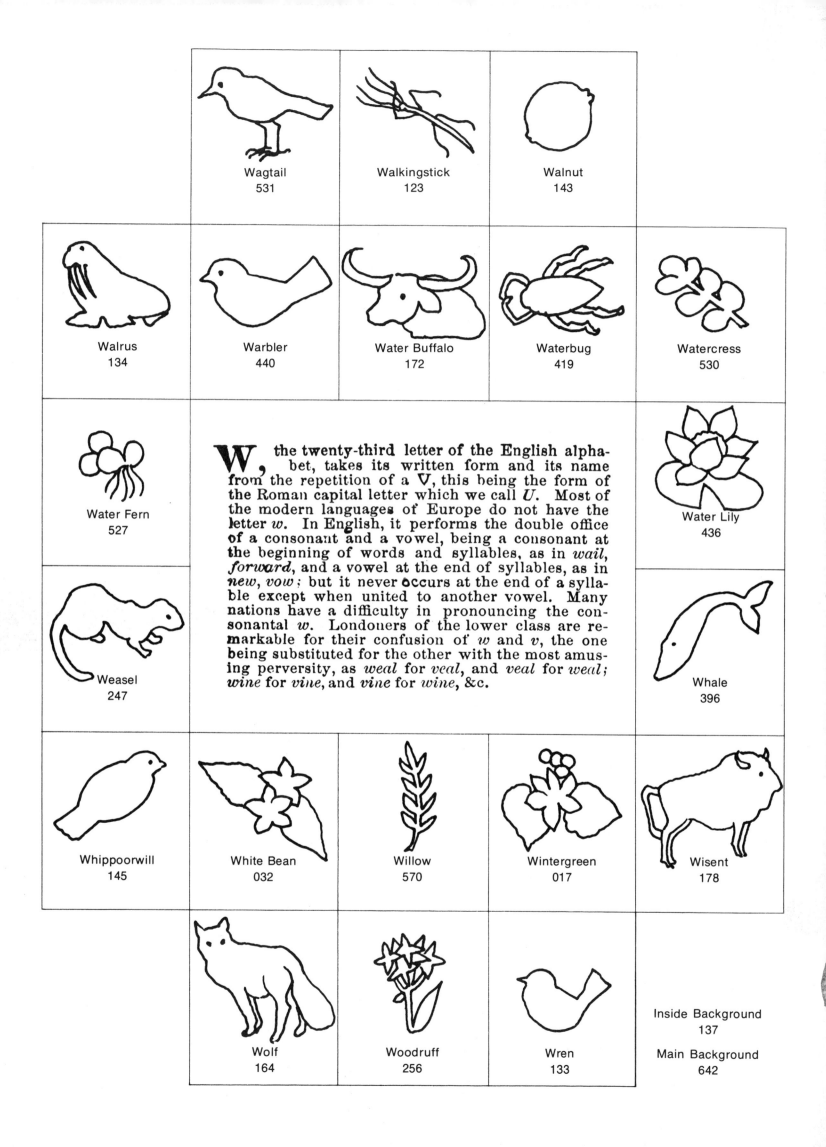

Wagtail
531

Walkingstick
123

Walnut
143

Walrus
134

Warbler
440

Water Buffalo
172

Waterbug
419

Watercress
530

Water Fern
527

Water Lily
436

Weasel
247

W, the twenty-third letter of the English alphabet, takes its written form and its name from the repetition of a **V**, this being the form of the Roman capital letter which we call *U*. Most of the modern languages of Europe do not have the letter *w*. In English, it performs the double office of a consonant and a vowel, being a consonant at the beginning of words and syllables, as in *wail, forward,* and a vowel at the end of syllables, as in *new, vow;* but it never occurs at the end of a syllable except when united to another vowel. Many nations have a difficulty in pronouncing the consonantal *w*. Londoners of the lower class are remarkable for their confusion of *w* and *v*, the one being substituted for the other with the most amusing perversity, as *weal* for *veal,* and *veal* for *weal; wine* for *vine,* and *vine* for *wine,* &c.

Whale
396

Whippoorwill
145

White Bean
032

Willow
570

Wintergreen
017

Wisent
178

Wolf
164

Woodruff
256

Wren
133

Inside Background
137

Main Background
642

Xanthium
570

Xanthoria
653

Xenophora
436

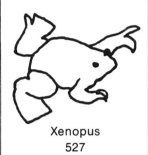

Xenopus
527

X, the twenty-fourth letter of the English alphabet, is borrowed, as to its form, from the Greek X. At the end of words, it has the sound of *ks*, as in *wax, lax*; in the middle, the sound of *ks*, or sometimes of *gz*, as in *axis, example, exhaust*. At the beginning of a word, it has the sound of *z*. See *Principles of Pronunciation*, § 104.

☞ Before the employment by the Greeks of their character Ξ or ζ, it was their common custom to represent this sound by X Σ rather than by K Σ. The Romans copied this Greek practice, and we consequently find in Latin inscriptions such forms as MAXSVMVS, PROXSVMVS, &c. But the Romans, being generally averse to the aspirated letters, had little or no occasion for the character X, except in this combination with an S. The very sight, therefore, of an X, even before the eye came to the S, raised in the mind the idea of a sibilant, and thus rendered the sibilant itself a superfluous letter, which, because it was superfluous, was before long omitted, and the single letter X made to perform the office of the two consonants X S.

Xenurus
531

Xerus
133

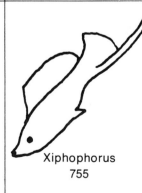

Xeranthemum
455

Xiphophorus
755

Xiphosura
178

Xylaria
017

Xylocopa
631

Xyris
550

Inside Background
137

Main Background
283

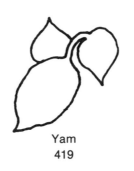

Yak
248

Yam
419

Yarrow
455

Yellow
550

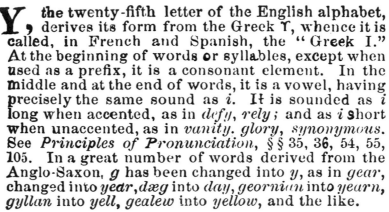

Y, the twenty-fifth letter of the English alphabet, derives its form from the Greek Υ, whence it is called, in French and Spanish, the "Greek I." At the beginning of words or syllables, except when used as a prefix, it is a consonant element. In the middle and at the end of words, it is a vowel, having precisely the same sound as *i*. It is sounded as *i* long when accented, as in *defy*, *rely*; and as *i* short when unaccented, as in *vanity. glory, synonymous*. See *Principles of Pronunciation*, §§ 35, 36, 54, 55, 105. In a great number of words derived from the Anglo-Saxon, *g* has been changed into *y*, as in *gear*, changed into *year*, *dæg* into *day*, *geornian* into *yearn*, *gyllan* into *yell*, *gealew* into *yellow*, and the like.

☞ *Y* has been called the *Pythagorean letter*, because its Greek original represents the sacred triad, formed by the duad proceeding from the monad; and also because it represents the dividing of the paths of vice and virtue in the development of human life. *Y* is used by ancient writers, especially Spenser, as a prefix of the past participle, used or omitted at will, and is also sometimes employed by modern writers in burlesque, or in imitation of the antique.

Yellow-Billed Cuckoo
440

Yellowhammer
447

Yellowjacket
960

Yellow Rattle
447

Yew
530

Yorkshire Terrier
134

Yucca
570

Inside Background
396

Main Background
659

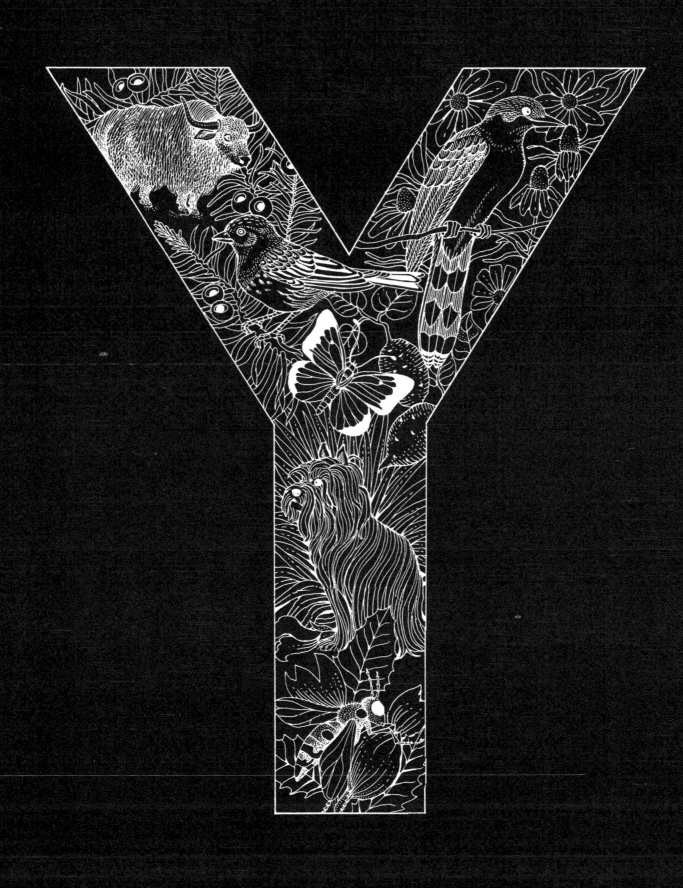

Zamia
530

Zanclas
419

Zebra
032

Zebra Plant
569

Zebu
178

Z. The twenty-sixth letter of the English alphabet, and the last letter in the alphabets of most modern languages. It is a sibilant consonant, and is merely a sonant or vocal s.

Zephyranthes
260

Zerynta
570

Zeus Dory
631

Zinnia
960

Zorilla
032

Zoysia
527

Zucchini
587

Zygaena
455

Inside Background
550

Main Background
631